Tell Me Why

WHY?

I See Falling Stars

Tamra B. Orr

Published in the United States of America by Cherry Lake Publishing
Ann Arbor, Michigan
www.cherrylakepublishing.com

Content Adviser: Matthew Linke, Planetarium Director, State Chair, Great Lakes Planetarium
Association (GLPA), University of Michigan Museum of Natural History Planetarium
Reading Adviser: Marla Conn, ReadAbility, Inc.

Library of Congress Cataloging-in-Publication Data

Orr, Tamra, author.
 I see falling stars / Tamra B. Orr.
    pages cm. -- (Tell me why)
  Summary: "Young children are naturally curious about the world around
them. I See Falling Stars offers answers to their most compelling questions
about meteors. Age-appropriate explanations and appealing photos encourage
readers to continue their quest for knowledge. Additional text features and
search tools, including a glossary and an index, help students locate
information and learn new words."—Provided by publisher.
  Audience: Ages 6-10.
  Audience: K to grade 3.
  Includes bibliographical references and index.
  ISBN 978-1-63188-996-7 (hardcover) -- ISBN 978-1-63362-035-3 (pbk.) --
ISBN 978-1-63362-074-2 (pdf) -- ISBN 978-1-63362-113-8 (ebook)
1. Meteors--Juvenile literature. 2. Meteorites--Juvenile literature. 3.
Children's questions and answers. I. Title.

 QB741.5.O77 2015
 523.5'1--dc23
                          2014031834

Cherry Lake Publishing would like to acknowledge the work of The Partnership for 21st Century
Skills. Please visit www.p21.org for more information.

Printed in the United States of America
Corporate Graphics

Table of Contents

Make a Wish!

Allison wheeled her bike into the garage. As she headed toward the house, she looked up and gasped. Right above her, **streaking** across the sky, was a falling star! She quickly closed her eyes and made a wish. Then she ran inside to tell everyone.

Nighttime is the best time to see bright lights in the sky.

"Hey!" she yelled. "Guess what I just saw outside?"

"A raccoon up in the tree?" asked her younger brother, Walsh.

"No!" said Allison. "I saw a falling star! It was right over my head. And yes, Walsh," she said before he could ask. "I made a wish."

What we think of as falling "stars" aren't actually stars at all.

"Why do stars fall in the first place, Dad?" Allison asked.

"And where do they go?" Walsh continued. "And are they really on fire? And how often does it happen?" His questions would have kept coming, but Dad put up his hand to stop him.

"Those are great questions. Let's take them one at a time."

Asking questions is a good way to learn, especially about the night sky.

Rocks on Fire

The Weber family gathered around the kitchen table. Dad began answering all of their questions.

"The first question you asked was why stars fall in the first place," he said. "Right, Ali?" She nodded. "My answer is that, despite their name, falling stars are not stars at all."

Falling stars are really pieces of rock, dust, or metal. They are usually made of **interplanetary** dust no bigger than a grain of sand or a tiny pebble. Occasionally, there are much bigger ones.

The bright streaks of light in the sky are not actually stars.

All of this outer-space **debris** races through the solar system at high speeds. Occasionally, some of this debris comes into contact with the atmosphere around Earth. The debris is moving so fast that it creates friction and begins to burn. This is when the debris becomes a **meteor**.

"So the flash of light you saw was a meteor," concluded Dad.

Millions of meteors come into Earth's atmosphere every day. Why do people only report seeing them at night?

As dust from space begins to burn, it can appear as a bright flash in the sky.

Falling to Earth

The Weber family went outside again to look at the night sky. Walsh spotted and pointed to a bright streak moving across the sky.

"Where does the meteor go?" he asked. "Does it hit the earth?"

"Most meteors burn up before they can reach the ground," explained Mom. "If one actually hits the planet before burning out, it is called a **meteorite**."

This is a meteorite—a piece of stony-iron called a pallasite.

Millions of pieces of space debris enter Earth's atmosphere daily. Only about 500 reach the ground. Most people would not recognize them. That's because most meteorites look much like rocks.

"Has a meteor ever fallen and hurt anyone?" asked Allison.

"Well, yes," their father said. "But it's very rare that someone is hurt by a falling meteor."

What do think happened to the meteorite that made this crater? Go online with an adult and learn more about it.

This is the Barringer Meteorite Crater in northern Arizona. It is the best-preserved crater on the planet.

Meteors on the Calendar

"I want to see more falling, um, meteors," said Allison. "Do I just come out every night and look?"

"There are better ways to do that," said Mom. "Astronomers can predict when there will be a **meteor shower**. In fact, one is coming next month."

LOOK!

Look closely at this photograph of a meteorite. Describe how it looks different from or the same as other rocks.

This meteorite, called the Hoba meteorite, is the largest single meteorite ever found on Earth.

Meteor showers are named for the **constellation** closest to where they appear to start from. Two of the biggest showers are the **Perseids** in mid-August and the **Leonids** in mid-November.

"Let's all get together next month to watch!" said Walsh.

Viewers of Perseids meteor showers may see 60 to 100 meteors an hour.

Think About It

If you were going to watch a meteor shower, what kind of place would be best? What would you bring with you?

Some people believe that the dinosaurs were killed long ago by a meteorite hitting the earth. Describe what you think might have happened.

In 2013, a large meteor raced across Russia's skies. It created shock waves and scared many people. Go online with an adult and see what scientists know about this meteor.

Glossary

constellation (kahn-stuh-LAY-shuhn) a group of stars

debris (duh-BREE) the pieces of something that has been destroyed or broken

interplanetary (in-tur-PLAN-i-tair-ee) occurring between planets or between the planet and the sun

Leonids (LEE-uh-nihdz) a shower of meteors occurring in the middle of November and near the constellation Leo

meteor (MEE-tee-ur) an object made of rock, dust, or metal entering Earth's atmosphere

meteor shower (MEE-tee-ur SHOU-er) an event in which many meteors can be seen at the same time

meteorite (MEE-tee-ur-rite) a meteor that hits the earth before burning up

Perseids (PUR-see-idz) a shower of meteors occurring in August and near the constellation Perseus

streaking (STREEK-eng) moving very fast

Find Out More

Books:

Lawrence, Ellen. *Comets, Meteors, and Asteroids: Voyagers of the Solar System*. New York: Ruby Tuesday Books, 2013.

Slahor, Dr. Stephenie. *Meteors*. Mechanicsburg, PA: Sunbury Press, 2013.

Woolf, Alex. *Meteor: Perspectives on Asteroid Strikes*. Mankato, MN: Heinemann-Raintree, 2014.

Web Site:

Kids Astronomy—Astronomy and Outer Space Games
   www.kidsastronomy.com/fun/index.htm
   Work a crossword puzzle, take an astronomy quiz, and play games at this site.

Index

About the Author

Tamra Orr is a full-time author who lives in Oregon. She has gotten to see a number of meteor showers, at least when the clouds get out of the way. She knows that falling stars are not really stars, but she still makes a wish whenever she sees one. She is a mom to four, a graduate of Ball State University, and the author of more than 350 books for readers of all ages.